(a) reduce the degree of discrimination, (b) inflate costs, and/or (c) increase production by selling output beyond output OX (Figure 8) at a price below marginal cost. Any of these alternatives will use up the excess profits.

If discrimination is reduced, AR (Figure 8) will shift to the left as profits are eliminated. When profits are completely dissipated, AR will coincide with D, and the Pareto optimal output (OX) will be obtained at the Pareto optimal price (OP). This alternative requires a voluntary transfer of surplus from the producer (or the general fund) to the consumer. Experience suggests that neither the management nor local officials are likely to adopt this alternative.

If discrimination is maintained, excess or unwanted profits may be used up in cost increasing activities including managerial emoluments, "services" to the community, and other fringe items. The management might develop a preference for expense which may be exceedingly difficult to control depending upon the amount of autonomy given to utility officials. This "expense preference" model eliminates unseemly profits without restricting output in the traditional monopoly sense and without reducing prices. The income transfer is a transfer from consumers to management. Needless to say, political patronage and political machines can be developed on the assumption of expense preference.

The third possibility is to increase the degree of discrimination by reducing marginal rates to a level below marginal cost. Thus, in Figure 8, the utility can expand output to OX_8 and eliminate profits completely by selling the segment XX_8 at a price below marginal cost. The plant is larger than optimum, and welfare, as measured by surplus, is reduced. That is, there is extreme overinvestment, and some customers are being charged what the traffic will bear while others are receiving bargain rates. This alternative reflects a managerial preference for a larger empire and would seem to be a more efficient device for political purposes than the expense preference model. This alternative is also consistent with the political practices of supplying some important commercial and industrial users with favorable rates, as well as providing the rationale behind low promotional rates and alleged economies derived from serving large users. This model takes on particular significance when related to municipally owned utilities because the objective of these utilities is not to raise as much revenue as possible. Most community officials have a relatively fixed sum of money they expect to receive from the utility for general fund revenues.

When this sum is acquired, any additional utility net revenue is considered undesirable. To avoid these excess revenues, the utility managers can carry out expansion of output at rates below cost to use up the revenue, such as the expansion into markets where costs are greater than revenues.[18]

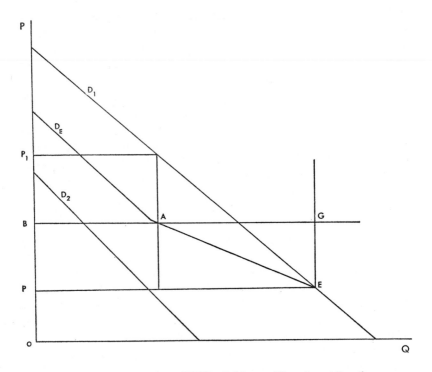

Fig. 9. An Interpretation of Utility Pricing and Investment Practices

An alternative model, which represents a variation of the quantity maximization or empire-building model, is shown in Figure 9 below. This model considers the general approach of utility managers which, from all indications, seems to be one of supplying the total quantity of water demanded at a price equal to short-run marginal (out-of-pocket) cost. The only form of rationing appears to be the ability of

13. Harvey Averch and Leland L. Johnson, "Behavior of the Firm Under Regulatory Constraint," *American Economic Review*, p. 1058. Also see Oliver E. Williamson, *The Economics of Discretionary Behavior: Managerial Objectives in a Theory of the Firm*; Milton Z. Kafoglis, "The Public Interest in Utility Rate Structures," undated manuscript.

water meters to handle a flow of water at any given point in time. The use of out-of-pocket cost pricing leads to a vast overexpansion of water facilities. In Figure 9, D_1 is the peak demand, D_2 the off-peak demand, and the utility operates under an assumption of constant costs. The same marginal price (OP) is charged to both the peak and off-peak users—a price equated with short-run marginal costs. Capacity is defined by point E where the peak demand intersects the short-run marginal cost function. Using the single price (OP), the firm incurs losses equal to 2 (BGEP). It is obvious that capacity is overexpanded since the economic solution requires a capacity defined by point A to be constructed where D_E intersects long-run marginal cost with a peak price of OP_1 and an off-peak price of OP. The total loss in welfare from setting both prices equal to out-of-pocket costs is equal to the area of the triangle AGE when compared to the optimal capacity defined by point A. This marginal solution is one of the worst possible alternatives for pricing and investment decisions. Since the utility takes losses by equating price with short-run marginal costs, the use of discrimination becomes the means by which these losses are recovered. This discrimination is reflected by the almost universal use of declining block pricing by larger utilities.

The ability to practice discrimination along with the fact that water utilities seem pressed continuously suggests that the alternative described in Figure 9—quantity maximization and short-run marginal cost pricing—may be a major source of aggravation in the municipal water supply picture.

Administrative Problems

The peak and off-peak models presented to this point have assumed that demands are independent of each other. It is this assumption that permits a differential between peak and off-peak rates to be used. The assumption is realistic when dealing with the problem of seasonal variations in water use because users are unable to shift their water use from the peak summer months to the off-peak winter months. However, this is not the case with respect to the hourly peak.

The demand for water on an hourly basis is much more sensitive to price differentials than is the seasonal demand since the two demands are no longer independent of each other. The demand for water during the hourly peak becomes a partial function of the off-peak price. Therefore, if price differentials are maintained, the previous peak period could become the off-peak period, and the previous off-peak period could become the peak period.[14] Alternatively, the problem of a shifting peak might be avoided through the use of a fixed charge. The same variable use charge can be applied to both hourly periods, but a minimum charge with no water allowance might be used to develop the rate differential. Due to the expense of metering equipment needed to measure hourly water use, a minimum fixed charge designed to collect the additional costs arising from the hourly peak demand can be based upon the size of the water meter the user selects—the larger the meter, the larger the charge.

SOME ALTERNATIVE SOLUTIONS

In light of the problems presented by interdependent demands, administrative considerations, and the lack of zone pricing, it has become necessary to incorporate efficiency pricing into a more practical framework. Through the use of fixed charges and the inclusion of zone pricing, a practical pricing policy can readily be implemented which enhances the economic efficiency of present water pricing practices.

A Fixed Charge Model

A model using the ability to congest as the basis for a fixed charge to recover customer costs and hourly peak capacity costs is shown in Figure 10 where D_N represents the net demand for water during the hourly peak. The demand is net demand over and above the seasonal peak demand and cannot be controlled through a variable charge because of the interdependency of the hourly demands and the related administrative problems. The function MC_C is the marginal customer costs associated with serving an individual customer for each equivalent five-eighths inch meter. The difference between MC_C and MC_S + MC_C is the estimated marginal congestion costs created by an equivalent five-eighths inch meter during the hourly peak. These costs are due primarily to pressure losses arising from the heavy demand placed upon the system capacity. However, they can be converted into money costs if they are interpreted as the additional costs the utility must incur to offset pressure losses arising from different quantities of equivalent five-eighths inch meters.[15] The price-output relation-

14. This phenomenon has been a major problem in the telephone industry where continuous attempts to diminish the peak have resulted only in shifting the peak, leading to chaos in rates which has become the subject of a significant and far-reaching investigation by the Federal Communications Commission.

15. Engineering studies should be able to make available the data necessary to obtain the estimated water use which will contribute to the hourly peak load

ship is OP price and OX quantity of equivalent five-eighths inch meters. The fixed charge is OP with OC the part being used to recover customer costs and CP the part designed to recover the marginal capacity costs imposed by an equivalent five-eighths inch meter during the hourly peak.

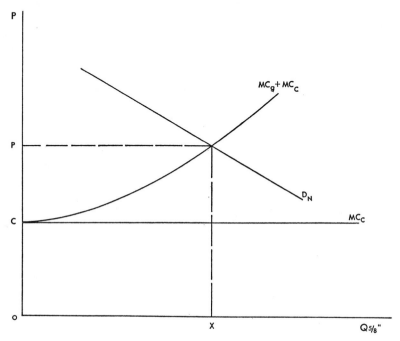

Fig. 10. Fixed Charge Based Upon the Ability to Congest the Water System

The user, at the time he selects the waterline needed for his purposes, is presented with the various meter sizes and their respective service charges. The user is then free to select the combination of meter size and service charge he desires, a choice which enables him to move to the preference level he desires. Due to present technological inefficiencies in water meters, a user cannot select a meter smaller than he

problem when different quantities of equivalent five-eighths inch meters are supplied. Discussions with water utility engineers has revealed and confirmed that although this data is not available, per se, at the present time, it can be developed from available data. Primarily, the records maintained about pressure losses along distribution mains combined with the distribution of equivalent five-eighths inch meters enable the development of congestion costs associated with different quantities of equivalent five-eighths inch meters.

needs in order to avoid a higher service charge and, then, attempt to run his water taps wide open during the peak period. Water pressure will drop, and, due to friction, the meter will record more water than is actually flowing through it. Consequently, the user gets lower quality service and pays for more water than he actually uses.

Because the capacity charge is fixed and not variable with water use, the user has no reason to shift his peak to other hours. Therefore, the utility is able to recapture hourly peak costs and avoid the problem of a shifting peak. In using a fixed charge, all customer costs and hourly peak capacity costs are put into the fixed charge, and the base water costs and seasonal extracapacity costs are allocated through a variable charge related to water use—a charge which is varied according to the month of the year.[16]

It should be noted that this model results in a solution which is welfare maximizing in the Williamson sense. The basic difference is that the model in Figure 10 assumes that congestion is an increasing function of the quantity of equivalent five-eighths inch meters while Williamson assumes that all costs are constant. The function $MC_g +$ MC_c is comparable to Williamson's long-run marginal cost function.[17]

Zone Pricing

One form of pricing which appears to be lacking in most of the solutions to water utility problems is zone pricing. The models have gener-

16. For excellent studies in the use of congestion pricing see the following articles: Clifton M. Grubs, "Theory of Spillover Cost Pricing," *Highway Research Record*, pp. 15–22; Herbert Mohring, "Relation Between Optimum Congestion Tolls and Present Highway User Charges," *Highway Research Record*, pp. 1–14; G. P. St. Clair, "Congestion Tolls—An Engineer's Viewpoint," *Highway Research Record*, pp. 66–112; A. A. Walters, "The Theory and Measurement of Private and Social Costs of Highway Congestion," *Econometrica*, pp. 676–99.

17. This solution eliminates the use of declining block-rate structures which are inefficient since their use entails different users paying a different price for the marginal unit, the cost of which is determined by the total amount of water taken during any given period. Since both users are marginal, each should be paying the same price. For studies which make some recommendations about rate structures see John Hopkinson, "On the Cost of Electric Supply," *The Development of Scientific Rates for Electric Supply*, pp. 5–20; Arthur Wright, "Cost of Electricity Supply," *The Development of Scientific Rates for Electric Supply*, pp. 31–52. A further modification should be noted when a waterborne sewage system is present. Part of this congestion may be attributed to such a system. Therefore, the congestion costs include water consumption, per se, along with disposal demand. For the cost allocation to be efficient, these congestion costs must be distributed between the water charge and the sewage charge. This allocation can be accomplished through the horizontal summation of the two demands. However, the solution becomes more complicated and somewhat less elegant.

ally concluded that in instances where there is excess capacity during the off-peak period, all capacity costs are to be paid by peak users. Since municipal water utilities tend to operate under such conditions, these conclusions suggest significant changes in water rate practices. However, the allocation of all capacity costs among peak users may not be the most efficient solution. It can be argued that some users should pay part of the capacity costs even though they use water only during the system's off-peak period, particularly in the case of distribution costs.[18] It is important to examine this argument.

Assume a utility serves three zones of which Zone A is one mile from the water plant, Zone B runs from one to two miles from the plant, and Zone C extends two to three miles from the water plant. Also assume the system peak occurs in period I, the peak in Zone A is in period I, the peak in Zone B is in period II, and the peak in Zone C is in period I. Given these assumptions, the utility is faced with a system peak in period I combined with a zone peak in period II in Zone B which is the sum of period II use in both Zones B and C. Under this arrangement, efficiency requires that all period I users contribute to the capacity costs in Zone A, i.e., all users in Zones A, B, and C. The capacity costs in Zone B (determined by period II users in Zones B and C) are allocated between the period II users in Zones B and C. Although these users are not consuming water during the system's peak, they are the users which determine the amount of capacity which must be placed in Zone B. Finally, the capacity in Zone C is allocated among the period I users in that zone because it is this use which determines the capacity in Zone C.

Under the arrangement described above, each user (zone) contributes to the capacity costs in accord with the water used during the peaks of the various zones. In this example, all zones contribute to the capacity costs in Zone A during the system peak. Zones B and C contribute to the capacity costs in Zone B in accordance with their peak use occurring in period II. Zone C is the only zone assessed for the capacity costs in Zone C.

The importance of zone pricing rests not only in the proper allocation of resources in water use. There is considerable significance with

18. Laurence C. Rosenberg, "Natural-Gas-Pipeline Rate Regulations: Marginal Cost Pricing and the Zone Allocation Problem," *Journal of Political Economy*, pp. 159–68. Also, many of these aspects are ably developed and put in a proper welfare perspective by M. Mason Gaffney, "Land and Rent in Welfare Economics," in *Land Economics Research*, eds. J. Ackerman, M. Clawson, and M. Harris, pp. 144–67.

respect to land use and other objectives. In a discussion of improper pricing policies tied to marginal rents and the constraints imposed by these rents, Gaffney makes the following point: "We have subsidized one after another new form of transportation, spreading thin the ground rent that otherwise would have concentrated about the older centers and mandated their intensive renewal. The result has been careless exploitation at the fringes, and stagnation at the cores. Periodically, the process has brought on stagnation at the fringes, also, as rents have collapsed following bursts of overexpansion. Low rents, recall, mean low constraints on the temporal extension of land uses, hence a freezing of capital turnover, and reduced employment of labor."[19]

A zone pricing solution can be used for rate differentials in both seasonal and daily peak load problems. The capacity costs during the seasonal peaks can be built into the variable use charge of each of the zones for each month of the year in accordance with use during the seasonal peak. The rate differentials can be used to reflect hourly peak and off-peak costs and the zones' relationship to the system hourly peak and off-peak demands. In the case of adjusting costs by zones, the resale of water to users in Zone B by users in Zone A, or the sale of water to users in Zone C by users in Zone B, can be prevented. The municipal water company is given a monopoly franchise to produce water for all three zones. Therefore, a user in Zone B, selling water to a user in Zone C (assuming the rates are lower in Zone B), puts himself into competition with the municipal water utility, an activity which is illegal under the terms of the franchise. Moreover, people in different zones, but adjacent to each other and trying to supply each other with water, can be checked through their water consumption. A user in Zone B supplying water to a user in Zone C would have an excessively low rate of water consumption as recorded by meter readings. Also, if a user in one zone attempts to take enough water to serve himself plus a neighbor in the next zone, a larger meter is required if the two users are to receive the same quality service as they received when both paid for their service separately. However, a larger meter requires a greater service charge to be paid by the user supplying the water because his ability to congest the system has been increased. If charges are appropriately established, this type of activity would not be profitable. The additional costs should offset any gains to both users.

Zone pricing can also be used to adjust rates in accordance with

19. "Land and Rent in Welfare Economics," p. 159.

cost differentials arising from such factors as geographical characteristics and population density.[20] The application is the same as the allocation of the capacity costs. These costs are assignable to each of the zones since a joint cost problem does not exist as is present in the peak and off-peak demand case. The optimal solution is that price-output relation which equates the effective demand in each zone with the long-run marginal costs of serving the zone. The long-run marginal costs of each zone include additional operating costs and the additional capacity costs—the additional capacity in the zone itself plus additional capacity which must be added to other zones.[21]

If a peak and off-peak demand are present in each of the zones, the pricing solution requires each period's price to be equated with the short-run marginal cost function. This application of zone pricing will represent an improvement in economic efficiency since the usual method for determining a single price for all zones (the usual present practice) is to take a weighted average of the costs in each zone and use this average as the single price. This alternative would lead to overexpansion in some zones where price is less than marginal costs and underexpansion in the zones where price is greater than marginal cost. Therefore, under present arrangements, the amount of capacity in any zone is not Pareto optimal unless some zone has costs equal to the average costs.[22]

20. Some further social problems and their solutions are discussed quite candidly by Gaffney. *Ibid.*, pp. 158–67.
21. This solution may be altered or modified by the presence of a waterborne waste disposal system. To the extent that part of the capacity is attributed to the disposal system, part of these costs should be allocated to the sewer charge and not to the water charge.
22. When three zones are served, it is assumed that the zones start at the site of the water plant and are served in succession, i.e., Zone A will be served before Zone B and Zone B before Zone C. However, if Zone C were to be served before Zone B, a joint supply problem seems to appear but such is not the case. To get service into Zone C, the utility must pass through Zone B, thus providing capacity to Zone B. However, if Zone B users were to take water, Zone C users would not receive service because of pressure losses. Greater capacity is needed through Zones A and B to serve both Zones B and C. The most likely solution is that the utility, upon passing through Zone B, will provide enough capacity in that zone so that it can be served in the future. Until service is actually provided in Zone B, Zones A and C will have to carry the costs of excess capacity in Zone B. However, the rates charged in Zone B can be set to provide a compensating subsidy to Zones A and C so that in the long run all zones pay a price equal to the additional costs of their service. If Zone B takes water without additional capacity being added, the prices in Zones B and C will have to be increased. The rate increases, *mutatis mutandis*, will be equal to the social costs of their congestion which will be equal

CONCLUSIONS

Through the use of economic analysis and the tools of welfare economics, it has been possible to develop theoretical models showing alternative solutions under various distributions of surplus. It was demonstrated that a single price monopoly solution results in the smallest plant capacity that can be rationalized from economic criteria. The use of first degree price discrimination results in the same output and total surplus as a competitive solution, but the distribution of the surplus must be judged on noneconomic criteria. The economics of block pricing were examined, and it was demonstrated that the number of blocks determines the proximity of actual capacity to the welfare maximizing capacity. However, it appeared that these models do not fully explain the techniques employed by municipal water utilities. Consequently, a model was developed to show the alternative of quantity maximization combined with out-of-pocket cost pricing as having greater relevance. The welfare implications of this alternative model were examined, and it was concluded that the welfare effects were some of the worst.[23]

To increase the general applicability of the theoretical models and to make the rate structures conform more closely to economic efficiency criteria, some adjustments in rate practices were suggested. The use of a net demand curve provides the means of establishing a fixed charge to overcome the problem of a shifting peak when hourly demands are relevant for pricing, while at the same time approaching a solution which is welfare maximizing in the Williamson sense. The fixed charge, based upon the meter size which measures the ability to congest the water system, provides the means of recovering the capacity costs which cannot be controlled through the use of prices because of the interdependency of demands, multiple price changes, and metering costs. The seasonal demands can be controlled through a variation in the variable charge as suggested by the economic models.

The use of zone pricing is recommended as a means of making rate

to the capacity costs of providing each zone with the proper amount of capacity to meet its demands where price is equal to long-run marginal cost.

23. The existence of a municipal sewage system and ordinances requiring the use of same may also account for some investment and output decisions which do not appear to have an economic basis when the water system itself is examined alone. In fact, if the waterborne waste disposal system is the primary determinant of capacity, it should carry all capacity costs. Any attempts to analyze the water system would lead to an overinvestment conclusion unless the sewer system is included.

structures conform more closely to efficiency criteria. Zone pricing enables rate structures to more accurately reflect marginal costs through the inclusion of demand characteristics, geographical characteristics, and population density. In short, the use of zone pricing better enables the attainment of the price equal to marginal cost criterion. The conclusion was also reached that, under certain conditions, users taking water during the system's off-peak might be required to pay part of the capacity costs.

However, in the case of municipally owned water utilities, distributive judgments are built into rate structures when utilities are placed in the entire framework of the community's revenue-expenditure budget. The problem becomes one of showing the efficiency implications of these distributive judgments and the means of financing deficits created by quantity maximization policies. These are the objectives underlying subsequent sections of this study. These alternative objectives represent marked departures from the goal of maximizing economic efficiency. However, before they can be properly evaluated a frame of reference must be provided against which the effects of the alternatives can be discerned. Therefore, it is essential that a theoretical basis be provided which relies on economic efficiency criteria for its justification. Then, these alternative objectives can be measured and understood in terms of their effects on economic efficiency.[24]

24. Much of the discussion to this point has inferred, either implicitly or explicitly, that an efficient solution requires the use of beneficiary charges. However, it has been argued recently that the relationship between such charges and optimal resource allocation is not a clear-cut issue. For a discussion of some of the issues involved, see William S. Vickery, "General and Specific Financing of Municipal Services," in *Readings in Welfare Economics*, eds. K. J. Arrow and T. Scitovsky, pp. 561–87.

6. Distributive Judgments
and Economic Efficiency

IT IS OBVIOUS THAT MUNICIPAL WATER utility officials do not adhere rigorously to economic efficiency criteria in the determination of utility rate structures. Rate policies do not (and perhaps should not) attempt to maximize welfare in the Paretian sense. Rate structures generally incorporate block pricing usually justified on a cost basis, but the cost criterion is primarily average or fully distributed costs.[1] Municipal water utilities make little or no use of rate differentials which reflect the different cost impacts of the peak and off-peak demands. However, it cannot be said that municipal water rate practices are founded on completely irrational criteria. There is a rationale for the rate practices that are pursued regardless of how irrational these criteria may appear to the theorist.

Municipal water revenue is one of several sources of revenue available to communities for financing municipal services. It is inevitable, therefore, that water rate structures will have some relationship to local financial and developmental policies. The concern over social objectives, such as tax efficiency, greater revenue, and community growth and development, requires distributive judgments about the financing of a municipal water utility and leads to rate practices that might deviate considerably from the criteria that have been developed in preceding sections.

The purpose of the present section is to demonstrate how distributive judgments might cause utility practices to depart from efficiency criteria and to demonstrate how economic analysis might provide some basic guidelines to preserve efficiency even though water rates may be manipulated to achieve some other social objective.

1. For excellent statewide surveys of municipal water utility practices see Georgia Municipal Association, *A Study of Municipal Water and Sewer Utility Rates and Practices in Georgia,* and Pennsylvania League of Cities, *Water Utility Operations.*

WATER RATES AND TAX POLICY

Many local communities frequently are forced to rely upon their water utility as a source of revenue for financing general fund expenditures because of: state preemption of income, sales, and other taxes; constitutional restrictions and other limitations on taxing powers; and local notions of tax equity. When a water utility is used for revenue purposes, water rates may incorporate a tax component. Therefore, the implications of the "tax" must be evaluated in the light of tax equity.

Two major alternative criteria for the attainment of tax equity are that each individual be taxed (a) in accordance with ability to pay, or (b) in accordance with benefits received. To be equitable, a tax should be levied in such a manner that those individuals with equal abilities to pay, or equal benefits received, pay equal taxes. As a corollary, those individuals with unequal abilities to pay, or receiving unequal benefits, should be taxed unequally.[2] Attempts to attain tax equity have led to some municipal water rate practices heretofore labeled as arbitrary or nonefficient.

Block Pricing and Taxation

General revenue (profit) was maximized when marginal revenue of the last block was equal to long-run marginal costs, and output was sold in blocks of equal size (assuming a straight line demand function). The amount of general revenue the community wants to derive from its water utility, then, determines the number of blocks built into the rate structure—the greater the desired level of revenue (the closer to perfect discrimination), given the demand functions, the greater the number of blocks. However, the character of the rate schedule has considerable impact on the distribution of the tax burden.

An allocation of the burden which falls heaviest upon large users might be used to place a large share of the "water-rate tax" upon individuals outside the community. In the case of industrial firms (the large water users), a relatively small percentage of their sales are to customers within the community's boundaries. Indeed, most sales will be in a multistate region outside the boundaries of the community. Therefore, in those instances where the large users bear the greatest relative revenue burden, the water tax might be passed on to their

2. For development of these points, see James M. Buchanan, *The Public Finances*, pp. 165–75; John F. Due, *Government Finance*, pp. 102–21.

customers via higher prices. However, the burden is shifted not to the residents of the community imposing the tax but on to outsiders. By avoiding intracommunity tax shifting, the municipality avoids the distributional effect of some users paying, through other higher prices, more than their allocated share of the burden of the water-rate tax.

A small number of blocks at the front of the schedule and few blocks at the end result in small users paying a relatively larger share of the revenue tax. This effect results from large users, having a greater proportion of their water use falling in the last block than small users, paying the lowest marginal and per-unit price. When this type of block structure is used, the tax burden is the most regressive because the burden falls on those uses with the most inelastic demand such as washing and laundering.[3] These uses, having the lowest demand elasticity, can present problems when they are taxed the heaviest. The rates might distribute the tax burden in a manner which conflicts with the ability to pay. However, if the community deems the most equitable basis for taxation is to charge what the traffic will bear, this rate structure is by definition the most equitable.[4] A second problem is setting rates on the first blocks so high that some very low income users might curtail their water consumption to levels below the amount considered necessary for minimum public health standards. In these instances, social costs and benefits become a relevant consideration in determining the rate structure.

When a community uses a single rate structure applied to all user classes (as suggested by efficiency criteria), all users pay the high per-unit prices of the early blocks in the rate schedule. However, revenue or tax objectives might justify different schedules for different user classes. Since a single rate schedule places a heavy burden on all users for their consumption of the first increment of water, the effect might

3. This type of schedule has been rationalized on economic grounds, and it has been concluded that the extracapacity costs, or demand charge, should be included in the first few blocks of the rate schedule. See Albert P. Learned, "Financial Problems of Municipally Owned Water Utilities," *JAWWA*, p. 1012; F. P. Linaweaver and John C. Geyer, "Use of Peak Demands in Determination of Residential Rates," *JAWWA*, p. 409. Also, most lawn sprinkling tends to occur in high income new suburban developments with large lots. The most stable loads are found in lower income older neighborhoods with small lots. These factors tend to indicate a situation where higher income groups receive a tax advantage over lower income groups.

4. Some writers feel that the criterion used by municipal water authorities for rate purposes is to charge what the traffic will bear. See Jerome W. Milliman, "The New Price Policies for Municipal Water Service," *JAWWA*, p. 127.

be a distribution of the tax burden which conflicts with the tax objectives used to determine the block sizes in the first place because no distinction is made between user classes. This problem may be avoided, however, by using a separate rate schedule for each class of user. In this manner, the burden of the revenue tax can be placed directly on those users for whom it was intended (assuming there is no shifting). The use of block schedules for each user class enables the community to better carry out the tax objectives of the water rate schedule in a manner which is both more efficient and more equitable than when a single rate schedule is applied to all classes. However, different rates to different classes involves the sacrifice of economic efficiency, is discriminatory pricing based upon noneconomic criteria, and should be recognized as such.

Problems Associated with the Use of a Water-Rate Tax

The use of a water-rate tax provides the only means available to some communities for raising additional revenues to finance ever expanding municipal needs, or for extracting taxes from county residents to be used to finance municipal expenditures from which county water users cannot be excluded, such as purely collective goods and quasi-collective goods. However, there are some serious drawbacks to this form of taxation which must be considered.

Implicit in this form of taxation is the assumption that the distribution of benefits, or the distribution of the ability to pay, is in proportion to the elasticity of demand for water. To the extent that this assumption is satisfied, the use of water bills as a form of taxation leads to an equitable distribution of the tax burden. However, it appears doubtful that these distributions do conform to the demand elasticity of water use, or to water bills calculated under a declining block-rate schedule. Therefore, a tax dependent upon elasticity, or the total water bill, will not conform to tax equity criteria. A more equitable tax might very well be one which is built into the fixed service charge rather than taxes built into declining block rates, per-unit taxes, or ad valorem taxes.

With the tax placed in the basic service charge, each water consumer makes a fixed contribution to the city's general fund revenues, and the tax is not one based upon elasticity. The amount of the tax included in the service charge can be based upon the proportion of other taxes each class of water user pays to the city, and thus achieve horizontal tax equity.[5] The use of this type of lump-sum tax will have

5. The city might estimate what proportion of its tax revenues comes from resi-

little impact upon water use, an important criterion for purposes of minimizing so-called excess burden.

A community is faced with a dilemma when using its water utility as a source of tax revenue. This dilemma arises between the use of water rates to achieve efficiency in resource use and the use of water rates for tax purposes. A per-unit tax on the quantity of water used, or an ad valorem tax which is directly related to water use, might have a significant impact upon water consumption because of the relative price elasticity of the lawn sprinkling demand. Therefore, a per-unit tax can be used to bring about a reduction in water use for efficiency purposes by rationing water when water scarcities exist. However, for tax purposes, a reduction in water consumption represents an erosion of the tax base which provides the source of revenues needed to finance general fund expenditures. Therefore, careful administrative judgment is required to reach a satisfactory compromise between the two alternative effects. On the other hand, the use of a fixed charge does not guarantee that each individual is being taxed in accordance with benefits received or his ability to pay. Each individual, contributing a fixed amount, might pay more or less than his benefits, or ability, depending upon the amount of his use of the collective good, or the size of his income. But the fixed charge does eliminate the need for a choice between restricting water use to economize water supply and expanding water use to create a greater tax base.

The Suburban Tax Problem

In many cases, the use of water-rate taxes provides the only means by which a community can reach suburban areas for tax purposes. Inside and outside water rate differentials usually are based upon the political boundaries of the community and the rationale behind this jurisdictional distinction is frequently costs. But, more importantly, the justification can be the attainment of tax equity and efficiency. It is generally recognized that those people living in adjacent suburbs receive benefits from central city expenditures on such services as parks and recreation, street improvements, mosquito control, hospitals, and, in some instances, educational facilities such as libraries. How-

---

dents, commercial businesses, and industries. These proportions can be applied to the total tax revenue the city wants to derive from the water users to estimate the share of the total water tax to be allocated to residential water rates, commercial rates, and industrial rates. The tax itself can then be put into the fixed service charge part of the water bill.

ever, these suburban beneficiaries are outside the taxing authority of the community. Thus, taxpayers residing inside the community may be subsidizing those taxpayers living in the suburbs. Attempts to reach these suburban taxpayers can be carried out readily through municipal water rates. The creation of water rate differentials between city and suburban users in excess of the cost differentials of serving the two groups is one means of obtaining some degree of tax equity based upon benefits received.[6] The grounds for a benefit tax can be justified by economic criteria if the benefits received by nontaxpaying suburban residents from a municipally provided quasi-collective good are necessary for the determination of the Pareto optimal price and quantity. If these benefits are not considered, the supply of the public good will be underexpanded.

Assume a community wishes to derive revenues from suburban users to finance a municipal service other than water. The supply of and demand for a quasi-collective good, such as mosquito control, provided by a central city government are shown in Figure 11.[7] The horizontal axis measures the quantity of city provided goods, D_1 measures the inside demand for the public good, and D_2 measures the outside demand for the good provided by the city.[8] At a price equal to marginal cost, inside city voters will vote for quantity OX_1.[9] However, since the good is available to county citizens, they will behave as though the good comes at a zero price. That is, quantity OX_3 will be demanded just by those county residents who are aware of a zero price. The Pareto optimal price relation is price OP_3 to city residents and price OP_2 to county residents. The Pareto optimal quantity is OX_2. If quantity OX_1 is retained, congestion develops, service quality deteriorates, and social marginal cost (SMC) increases. Consequently,

6. In some cases, the suburban residents can be excluded from receiving benefits by exclusion from the facility. This exclusion is done in some communities by restricting the use of parks, golf courses, and city dumps to the residents of the community. Admission is based on the place of residence. However, the exclusion cannot be accomplished in the case of purely collective goods, such as street improvements, police protection, and mosquito control. The suburban residents cannot be excluded from the use of the service or the derivation of any benefits from the service.

7. A purely collective good is one whose consumption by one individual does not diminish the total available to other individuals. See Paul A. Samuelson, "The Pure Theory of Public Expenditure," *Review of Economics and Statistics*, pp. 387–89.

8. For a careful discussion of the demand and cost curves for a collective good, see James M. Buchanan, *Public Finance in Democratic Process*, pp. 11–17.

9. For this voting process, see *ibid.*, pp. 11–17, 144–68.

both county and city residents reduce their use (or consumption) of the facility until, at quantity OX_1, a voluntary adjustment is reached. But, in this equilibrium, the county residents have driven off some of the city residents. Therefore, solution OX_1 is one where the city residents pay for the facility, both city and county residents use the

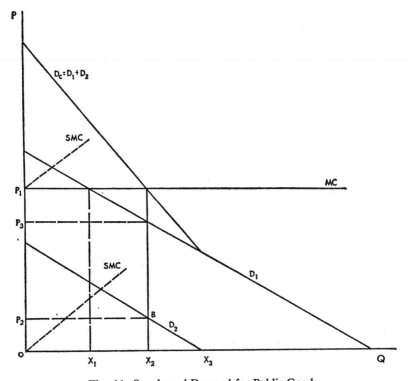

Fig. 11. Supply and Demand for Public Goods

facility, and there is congestion which results in either a reduction in the use of the facility or a deterioration in the quality of the service provided by the facility. That is, both classes get inferior service, and the city residents pay for both. This result is in serious conflict with the Pareto optimal quantity OX_2 which requires both county and city residents to share the costs. Although congestion at quantity OX_2 may be difficult to avoid since both groups behave as though the use price is zero, equity is improved and facilities expanded if the county residents pay for part of the facilities.

Given an amount of dollars equal to the rectangle P_2BX_20 (Figure 11), which is the amount of tax revenue to be derived from the county residents, how can this revenue be collected from county residents? The problem is one of institutionalizing the county payment. The payment, through the use of the water utility, can be extracted by: (1) setting outside rates so that utility operations are more profitable in the county than they are in the city; (2) using an ad valorem tax on the water bills of the county residents; (3) using a per-unit tax on the water consumed by county residents; and/or (4) using a fixed service charge tax.[10]

Industrial Location

Another primary concern of many communities is creating a local environment conducive to the economic growth of the community. The problems that have to be overcome are many, and frequently local communities attempt their solutions to these problems through their municipal water rate policies. Smaller communities, although not to the exclusion of larger communities, are faced with a deterioration in their property tax base, and further property tax increases may tend to enhance further deterioration. To encourage business location and reverse this tendency, these communities turn to their water utility. It is this attempt which explains, in part, some of the irrational rate practices which combine nonmarginal rate patterns, in some instances, with marginal provisions, in other instances. The rate schedule is often constructed so that the last blocks, which are of concern to businesses, have prices below marginal costs, and consequently the utility provides industry with water services at rates below cost.

There appears to be an economic rationale for such low rates to industrial users. Many industries will be given other location incentives such as exemption from personal property taxes and/or partial exemption from real property taxes. Municipal water rates might be used by the community to recover tax concessions through a readjustment of the blocks in the water rate schedule. In order to avoid this possibility, industries legitimately might require a community to give it

10. Studies of these alternatives within a broader context, to measure the impacts of each alternative, have been done by William J. Baumol, *Business Behavior, Value and Growth*, pp. 1–79, and Richard A. Musgrave, *The Theory of Public Finance*, pp. 276–311. Work on the impacts of a profit restraint on welfare is presently being done by Dr. Milton Z. Kafoglis in the Department of Economics at the University of Florida. For specifics see Milton Z. Kafoglis, "Output of the Restrained Firm," *American Economic Review*, pp. 583–89.

preferential water rates with a guarantee that rates will not be increased. Thus, there is some indication that large users can be sensitive to water charges although these costs might be only a small part of their total costs.

When tax concessions are given, someone has to bear the burden of the losses the utility incurs in the water sales to these large users. The losses can be pushed onto rates in the first blocks of the schedule so that water is sold at a price above marginal cost to many users—a practice which is consistent with the quantity maximization and out-of-pocket cost pricing model developed in the preceding section. When such pricing practices are carried out, the utility tends to overexpand, price of the marginal unit taken by small users is greater than marginal costs, and the price of the marginal unit taken by large users is below marginal costs. Efficiency can be improved by lowering prices and increasing the quantity available to small users and raising prices and reducing quantity available to large users. The net effect is a reduction in capacity.

The use of zone pricing in the rate structure can foster the development of industrial areas within the area. Setting up special industrial water systems, such as Savannah, Georgia, or preferential rates in given areas can encourage firms to locate in those areas where industry is desired. Furthermore, the direction of the expansion pattern in water service can effect the desired development pattern. Industry tends to follow the available sources of water. It follows, then, that when a community wants industry located in a specific area, water service must be supplied in that area. The expansion of the service can be accompanied with preferential water rates in that area. However, the losses incurred from this development and below-cost water rates must be borne by other taxpayers through either above-cost water rates or increased taxes in some other form such as property taxes.

Since these forms of industrial location incentives involve intra-community subsidies, they also involve a redistribution of surplus. Therefore, to meet the criterion that each change must be evaluated in terms of its implications on both economic efficiency and surplus distribution, a complete cost-benefit analysis is required. Only in this manner can a rational decision be reached regarding the relationship between marginal gains and marginal losses to the community. Furthermore, such analysis enables the judgment of whether or not the distribution of the burden of the incentive program conforms to standards of social equity the community may establish.

Community Development

Through the use of zone pricing, rate structures can not only encourage industrial location in the manner described above, but they can also influence the direction of economic development within a community. Water rates, adjusted by various zones, can be used to achieve long-run development plans of a community's long-range comprehensive plan. Areas in which development is to be encouraged can be given surplus benefits from low water rates or special services. The type of development to be encouraged, of course, determines the class of rates to be given preferential treatment in each zone.

If the community has a given area in which it wants to encourage residential development, low promotional rates to residential users can be offered while other users, such as commercial and industrial users, might be required to pay high penalty rates for locating in the same area. Alternatively, if the desire is to develop the area commercially, then this class of users can be given the preferential below-cost rates. The losses can be recovered from other classes of users (residential and industrial) whose presence in the area is to be discouraged or from other commercial users located in areas designated for residential or industrial development.

This form of development program involves intracommunity subsidies being paid from those users paying the above-cost rates to those users paying the below-cost rates. However, when the analysis goes beyond the realm of private costs and benefits and into the world of social costs and benefits, an economic justification for such practices evolves. In the examples cited above, it can be interpreted legitimately that nonconforming users are paying a form of social cost because they have located in an area in which their presence does not conform to the wishes of the society in which they operate. Therefore, those cases where price is less than marginal private cost to users in zones in which their development is being encouraged do not always imply that efficiency is being sacrificed. The relationship which is being satisfied is the following: marginal private benefits + marginal social benefits = marginal private costs + marginal social costs. Although marginal private benefit (price) is less than marginal private cost, the deficit may be very well equal to surplus of marginal social benefits over marginal social costs. Consequently, economic efficiency is enhanced by such pricing practices. Conversely, those users paying a price in excess of marginal private costs may not be paying an unwarranted rate subsidy. Since these users have located in zones in which they are not wanted, thereby making themselves nonconforming users, there are obvious social costs involved in their location decision. Therefore, when price is in excess of marginal private benefit, the difference can be offset by an excess of marginal social cost over marginal social benefit. Consequently, when users are paying a price equal to marginal private costs plus net social costs (marginal social cost minus marginal social benefits), the welfare of the community is being maximized.

As a brief summary remark, it has become obvious that some communities use their water rate schedules to effect some desirable settlement pattern within the community. Frequently, this practice is criticized on the grounds that subsidies are being paid by one class of user to another class of user. Once the word subsidy is used, the usual conclusion is that someone receives unfair treatment as a result of the utility manager's arbitrary judgment or pressure from special interest groups. Consequently, these rate practices are branded irrational. However, when social costs and benefits are incorporated into the analysis, some economic significance can be attached to this practice. However, an interesting area for future research is an examination of how close such practices come to the equating of social and private costs with social and private benefits.

Conclusions

Municipal water utilities provide a means of achieving community objectives such as tax equity and efficiency, and community growth and development. Such objectives, however, sometimes lead to rate practices which appear to be irrational—at least in terms of strict economic criteria. Relevant economic models, which equate marginal cost with price, apply criteria for efficiency and welfare maximization which are applicable to privately owned utilities. However, the municipally owned water utility serves other purposes than supplying water in the most efficient manner; therefore, distributive judgments are built into water rates as local government officials attempt to achieve these public oriented goals. Although social objectives may justify such practices, the alternatives must be weighed against these practices. That is, what alternative means exist (such as property taxes) to achieve the same objective and which is the best from a welfare standpoint?

It was shown that the construction of a block-rate structure, the usual form of water pricing, has significant distributional implications. Tax purposes, however, may require different rate schedules for different users, whereas economic criteria require all users to pay the same price. The water utility also provides a means by which a city government may reach county residents for tax revenues to be used in providing facilities from which county residents cannot be excluded from receiving benefits.

Implications in the use of water rates as taxing devices should be noted. The use of water bills as the basis for a tax effectively taxes individuals in proportion to their elasticity of demand for water. Consequently, large users may pay a relatively smaller share of the tax burden than small users because of the nature of block-rate structures.

The uses of water rates as a means of carrying out programs of community growth and development were examined, and the effects of water rates on the type and direction of industrial location and community development were shown.

When social objectives and their inherent distributive judgments are examined within the utility's role in the overall social objectives of a community, practices which at first appear to be irrational turn out to have some social rationale, regardless of how vain these rationales may be. This section has presented, to a limited extent, the economic and welfare consequences of various distributive judgments in the rate structure, an analysis seemingly totally absent in the literature of both economics and utility management.

7. Recommendations

Economic efficiency is concerned with the attainment of that allocation of resources, or input-output mix, which maximizes the satisfaction of the consumers in the economy. This efficiency criterion requires each water user to pay a price which reflects the marginal cost he imposes, assuming, of course, there are no complications stemming from joint supply, interdependent demands, externalities, and distributional objectives in conflict with economic efficiency.

It is obvious that water rates are not constructed in a manner designed to achieve welfare maximization, at least in the Paretian context. The apparent use of quantity maximization coupled with strong price discrimination leads to a vast overexpansion in capacity and a system of internal cross-subsidies that may aggravate the distributional problem.

For a municipally owned water utility to properly evaluate the economic efficiency and distributional impacts of its rate practices, it is helpful to derive pricing guidelines based on efficiency criteria with distributional judgments temporarily put aside. This basic model can provide a standard of comparison for determining the distributional effects of rate practices based on efficiency criteria, the efficiency effects of rate practices based on distributional judgments, and the distributional effects of equity judgments built into the rate structures. This type of analysis is extremely important in the case of municipally owned water utilities since, in their operation, economic efficiency and distributional equity are traded off as the two come into conflict. The model should be one which is based upon a set of assumptions which fit the conditions under which a water utility provides service. These conditions are independent demands between seasonal peak and off-peak periods, interdependency between hourly peak and off-peak demands, and joint costs between both seasonal and hourly peak and off-peak periods.

In the hope that water rate practices might conform more closely to economic efficiency (as well as becoming more equitable), several pricing guidelines have been recommended.

In the case of independent demands, the Williamson model provides an optimal solution in terms of economic efficiency. His model entails equating the effective demand for capacity with long-run marginal costs to determine plant capacity and the off-peak price with short-run marginal cost (when the off-peak demand fails to utilize capacity at this price). The peak price is determined so that the quantity demanded is equated to the capacity to produce (assuming an indivisibility constraint).

The pricing scheme established by Williamson should be extended to take into consideration the costs of supplying various zones. This guideline can be used to determine the optimal level of capacity the utility should provide in each zone. The effective demand for capacity of each zone is equated with the long-run marginal costs in each zone. These additional costs include additional production costs, additional capacity costs in the zone itself, and additional capacity costs which must be placed in other zones as a result of additional service provided to the zone in question.

When demands are interdependent, administrative problems arise which complicate the use of rate differentials to achieve economic efficiency. However, the utility may, through the use of a fixed charge, overcome these problems and recover the cost differences of serving the hourly peak and off-peak users. The capacity costs can be estimated from engineering data which indicate the load imposed by various quantities of equivalent five-eighths inch meters. By using an average daily demand and the amount of actual water production during the peak hour, the additional capacity required to meet the hourly peak demand over and above the seasonal peak demand can be determined. These additional costs can then be incorporated into a service charge which does not include water usage. The level of the charge is determined on the basis of the number of equivalent five-eighths inch meters each user takes which bases the charge upon the user's ability to congest the water system during the system's peak load and allows the user to select his own meter size and accompanying charge, thus, his own preference level. This alternative is also recommended as an alternative to metering hourly water use which involves, at the present time, a level of costs so high that any gains in efficiency would probably be more than offset by additional costs.

The fixed charge will not alter the pattern of water use, but it will avoid the administrative problems associated with shifting peaks. There is no incentive for users to shift their peak use over into hours which are, at the present time, the off-peak hours; the individual has the freedom to select the amount of capacity he needs; and the utility has the ability to determine the degree of peak load capacity it must provide. This service charge includes both customer costs and extra-capacity costs required to serve the hourly peak.

A variable use charge can be designed to recover base water costs and extracapacity costs incurred in serving the seasonal demand. The costs included in the variable charge should be spread evenly throughout the rate schedule with each user paying the same marginal price. The total contribution of each user toward capacity costs, therefore, is proportional to the total quantity of water used. Consequently, block-rate structures (price discrimination) should not be used if efficiency is the primary criterion. However, block rates might be employed when overriding social considerations entail the use of the utility as a revenue raising device, as a means of achieving some form of tax distribution, or as a means of promoting community development. But, the rate analysts should be aware of the many distributional effects of such rate practices.

The basic water charge should not include a water usage because the effect of such allowances is to provide water to some users on the basis of an effective flat monthly charge which entails elaborate bounties and cross-subsidies along with the inequality between price and marginal cost.

The use of zone pricing and rate differentials might also be used to encourage industrial location and intracommunity development which can enhance community growth and prevent slum development. In these instances, some sacrifice of pure economic efficiency must be made to encourage some other social goals. However, social costs and benefits become an important consideration, and they must be considered along with private costs and benefits to determine a social optimum.

An important consideration in the design of rate structures is the ability of the consumer to understand the basis for his water bill and the administrative costs of supplying such information. A water rate schedule which is highly technical because of its adherence to strict economic efficiency pricing can lead to user resistance and complaints about water bills. Moreover, the effect is to increase the administrative costs of handling billing, as numerous bills must be explained and recomputed to satisfy customer complaints. Although overall efficiency might be increased by using a more simplified rate policy, the argument for simplicity, which must not be overlooked, is frequently employed to justify what in reality is an inequitable and inefficient rate structure.

Bibliography

Books

Arrow, Kenneth J. *Social Choice and Individual Values.* New York: John Wiley and Sons, 1951.

Baumol, William J. *Business Behavior, Value and Growth.* Rev. ed. New York: Harcourt, Brace and World, 1967.

————. *Economic Theory and Operations Analysis.* 2nd ed. Englewood Cliffs: Prentice-Hall, 1965.

————. *Welfare Economics and the Theory of the State.* 2nd ed. Cambridge: Harvard University Press, 1965.

Bergson, Abram. *Essays in Normative Economics.* Cambridge: Harvard University Press, 1966.

Bonavia, Michael R. *The Economics of Transport.* New York: Pitman Publishing Corp., 1936.

Boulding, Kenneth E. *Economic Analysis: Microeconomics.* New York: Harper and Row, 1966.

Buchanan, James M. *Public Finance in Democratic Process.* Chapel Hill: University of North Carolina Press, 1967.

————. *The Public Finances.* Homewood: Richard D. Irwin, 1960.

Clemens, Eli. *Economics and Public Utilities.* New York: Appleton-Century, 1960.

Davidson, Ralph K. *Price Discrimination in Selling Gas and Electricity.* Baltimore: Johns Hopkins University Press, 1955.

Due, John F. *Government Finance.* 3rd ed. Homewood: Richard D. Irwin, 1963.

Graaff, J. de V. *Theoretical Welfare Economics.* Cambridge: Cambridge University Press, 1963.

Hicks, John R. *A Revision of Demand Theory.* London: Oxford University Press, 1956.

————. *Value and Capital.* 2nd ed. Oxford: Oxford University Press, 1946.

Hirshleifer, Jack, James C. DeHaven, and J. W. Milliman. *Water Supply.* Chicago: University of Chicago Press, 1960.

Kafoglis, Milton Z. *Welfare Economics and Subsidy Programs* (University of Florida Monographs: Social Sciences, No. 11). Gainesville: University of Florida Press, 1961.

Lerner, Abba P. *The Economics of Control.* New York: Macmillan Co., 1944.

Little, I. M. D. *A Critique of Welfare Economics.* Oxford: Oxford University Press, 1958.

Locklin, D. Philip. *Economics of Transportation.* 6th ed. Homewood: Richard D. Irwin, 1966.

Marshall, Alfred. *Principles of Economics*. 8th ed. London: Macmillan and Co., Ltd., 1920.

Musgrave, Richard A. *The Theory of Public Finance*. New York: McGraw-Hill Book Co., 1959.

Pigou, A. C. *The Economics of Welfare*. 4th ed. London: Macmillan and Co., Ltd., 1932.

Reder, A. *Studies in the Theory of Welfare Economics*. New York: Columbia University Press, 1947.

Samuelson, Paul A. *Foundations of Economic Analysis*. New York: Atheneum, 1965.

Smith, Adam. *The Wealth of Nations*. New York: Random House, Modern Library, 1937.

Stigler, George J. *The Theory of Price*. Rev. ed. New York: The Macmillan Co., 1962.

Vickery, William S. *Microstatics*. New York: Harcourt, Brace and World, 1964.

Williamson, Oliver E. *The Economics of Discretionary Behavior: Managerial Objectives in a Theory of the Firm*. Englewood Cliffs: Prentice-Hall, 1964.

Articles

Averch, Harvey, and Leland L. Johnson. "Behavior of the Firm Under Regulatory Constraint," *American Economic Review* 52 (December, 1962): 1052–69.

The American Water Works Association. "The Water Utility Industry in the United States," *Journal of the American Water Works Association* 58 (July, 1966): 772–76.

Baxter, Samuel S. "Principles of Rate Making for Publicly Owned Utilities," *Journal of the American Water Works Association* 52 (October, 1960): 1225–38.

Bergson, Abram. "A Reformulation of Certain Aspects of Welfare Economics," *Quarterly Journal of Economics* 52 (February, 1938): 310–34.

Boiteux, Marceo. "La Tarification des Demands en Pointe: Application de la Theórie de la Vent au Côut Marginal," trans. H. W. Izzard, in *Marginal Cost Pricing in Practice*, ed. James R. Nelson. Englewood Cliffs: Prentice-Hall, 1964, pp. 59–89.

Bonbright, J. C. "Fully Distributed Costs in Utility Rate Making," *American Economic Review* 51 (May, 1961): 305–12.

———. "Major Controversies as to the Criteria of Reasonable Public Utility Rates," *American Economic Review* 30 (May, 1940): 379–89.

———. "Two Partly Conflicting Standards of Reasonable Utility Rates," *American Economic Review* 48 (May, 1957): 386–93.

Bonine, E. D. "Making a Water Utility Solvent," *Journal of the American Water Works Association* 45 (May, 1953): 457–58.

Boulding, Kenneth E. "Welfare Economics," in *A Survey of Contemporary Economics*, vol. 2, ed. Bernard F. Haley. Homewood: Richard D. Irwin, 1952, pp. 1–38.

Buchanan, James M. "Peak Loads and Efficient Pricing: Comment," *Quarterly Journal of Economics* 80 (August, 1966): 463–71.

Faust, Raymond J. "The Needs of Water Utilities," *Journal of the American Water Works Association* 51 (June, 1959): 701–6.

Fisher, Gordon P. "New Look at Resources Policy," *Journal of the American Water Works Association* 57 (March, 1965): 255–61.

Fox, Irving K., and Orris C. Herfindahl. "Attainment of Efficiency in Satisfying Demands for Water Resources," *American Economic Review* 54 (May, 1964): 198–206.

Gaffney, M. Mason. "Land and Rent in Welfare Economics," in *Land Economics Research,* eds. J. Ackerman, M. Clawson, and M. Harris. Washington: Resources for the Future, 1962, pp. 144–67.

Grubs, Clifton M. "Theory of Spillover Cost Pricing," in *Highway Research Record* No. 47. Washington: Highway Research Board, 1964, pp. 15–22.

Hatcher, Melvin P. "Basis for Rates," *Journal of the American Water Works Association* 57 (March, 1965): 273–78.

Hicks, John R. "The Foundations of Welfare Economics," *Economic Journal* 49 (December, 1939): 696–712.

————. "The Four Consumer Surpluses," *Review of Economic Studies* 11 (1943): 68–74.

————. "The Generalized Theory of Consumer's Surplus," *Review of Economic Studies* 13 (1945–46): 68–74.

————. "The Rehabilitation of Consumers' Surplus," *Review of Economic Studies* 8 (February, 1941): 108–16.

Hirshleifer, J., and J. W. Milliman. "Urban Water Supply: A Second Look," *American Economic Review* 57 (May, 1967): 169–78.

Hopkinson, John. "On the Cost of Electric Supply," in *The Development of Scientific Rates for Electric Supply.* Detroit: The Edison Illuminating Co., 1915, pp. 5–20.

Hotelling, Harold. "The General Welfare in Relation to Problems of Taxation and of Railway and Utility Rates," *Econometrica* 6 (July, 1938): 242–69.

Howson, Louis R. "Review of Ratemaking Theories," *Journal of the American Water Works Association* 58 (July, 1966): 849–55.

Kafoglis, Milton Z. "Output of the Restrained Firm," *American Economic Review* 59 (September, 1969): 583–89.

Kaldor, Nicholas. "Welfare Propositions of Economics and Interpersonal Comparisons of Utility," *Economic Journal* 49 (September, 1939): 549–52.

Keller, Charles W. "Design of Water Rates," *Journel of the American Water Works Association* 58 (March, 1966): 293–99.

Learned, Albert P. "Determination of Municipal Water Rates," *Journal of the American Water Works Association* 49 (February, 1957): 165–73.

————. "Financial Problems of Municipally Owned Water Utilities," *Journal of the American Water Works Association* 50 (August, 1958): 1009–13.

Linaweaver, F. P., and John C. Geyer. "Use of Peak Demands in Determination of Residential Rates," *Journal of the American Water Works Association* 56 (April, 1964): 403–13.

Machlup, Fritz. "Theories of the Firm: Marginalist, Behavioral, Managerial," *American Economic Review* 57 (March, 1967): 1–33.

Meyer, John R., and Gerald Kraft. "The Evaluation of Statistical Costing Techniques as Applied in the Transportation Industry," *American Economic Review* 51 (May, 1961): 313–34.

Milliman, Jerome W. "The New Price Policies for Municipal Water Service," *Journal of the American Water Works Association* 56 (February, 1964): 125–31.

Mohring, Herbert. "Relation Between Optimum Congestion Tolls and Present Highway User Charges," in *Highway Research Record* No. 47. Washington: Highway Research Board, 1964, pp. 1–14.

Nelson, J. R. "Practical Applications of Marginal Cost Pricing in the Public Utility Field," *American Economic Review* 53 (May, 1963): 474–81.

Patterson, William L. "Practical Water Rate Determination," *Journal of the American Water Works Association* 54 (August, 1962): 904–12.

Pigou, A. C. "Railway Rates and Joint Costs," *Quarterly Journal of Economics* 27 (May, 1913); 535–36.

———. "Railway Rates and Joint Costs," *Quarterly Journal of Economics* 27 (August, 1913): 687–92.

Rosenberg, Laurence C. "Natural-Gas-Pipeline Rate Regulations: Marginal Cost Pricing and the Zone Allocation Problem," *Journal of Political Economy* 75 (April, 1967): 159–68.

Ruggles, Nancy. "Recent Developments in the Theory of Marginal Cost Pricing," *Review of Economic Studies* 17 (1949–50): 107–26.

———. "The Welfare Basis of the Marginal Cost Pricing Principle," *Review of Economic Studies* 17 (1949–50): 31.

St. Clair. G. P. "Congestion Tolls—An Engineer's Viewpoint," in *Highway Research Record* No. 47. Washington: Highway Research Board, 1964, pp. 66–112.

Samuelson, Paul A. "The Pure Theory of Public Expenditure," *Review of Economics and Statistics* 36 (November, 1954): 387–89.

———. "Welfare Economics and International Trade," *American Economic Review* 28 (June, 1938): 259–72.

Scitovsky, Tibor. "A Note on Welfare Propositions in Economics," *Review of Economic Studies* 9 (1941–42): 77–88.

———. "Two Types of Externalities," *Journal of Political Economy* 62 (April, 1954): 143–51.

Shepherd, William G. "Marginal Cost Pricing in American Utilities," *Southern Economic Journal* 23 (July, 1966): 58–70.

Steiner, Peter O. "Peak Loads and Efficient Pricing," *Quarterly Journal of Economics* 71 (November, 1957): 585–610.

Taussig, F. W. "Railway Rates and Joint Costs Once More," *Quarterly Journal of Economics* 27 (February, 1913): 378–85.

———. (Untitled Rebuttal to A. C. Pigou), *Quarterly Journal of Economics* 27 (May, 1913): 536–38.

———. (Untitled Rebuttal to A. C. Pigou), *Quarterly Journal of Economics* 27 (August, 1913): 692–93.

Troxel, Emory. "Incremental Cost Determination of Utility Rates," *Journal of Land and Public Utility Economics* 18 (1942): 458–67.

Vickery, William S. "General and Specific Financing of Municipal Services," in *Readings in Welfare Economics*, eds. K. J. Arrow and T. Scitovsky. Homewood: Richard D. Irwin, 1969, pp. 561–87.

———. "Some Implications of Marginal Cost Pricing for Public Utilities," *American Economic Review* 45 (May, 1955): 605–20.

———. "Some Objectives to Marginal Cost Pricing," *Journal of Political Economy* 56 (June, 1948): 218–38.

Wallace, Donald H. "Joint Supply and Overhead Costs and Railway Rate Policy," *Quarterly Journal of Economics* 48 (August, 1934): 583–619.

Walters, A. A. "The Theory and Measurement of Private and Social Costs of Highway Congestion," *Econometrica* 29 (October, 1961): 676–99.

Williamson, Oliver E. "Peak-Load Pricing and Optimal Capacity Under Indivisibility Constraint," *American Economic Review* 56 (September, 1966): 810–27.

Winch, David M. "Consumer's Surplus and the Compensation Principle," *American Economic Review* 55 (June, 1965): 395–423.

Wright, Arthur. "Cost of Electric Supply," *The Development of Scientific Rates for Electric Supply*. Detroit: The Edison Illuminating Co., 1915, pp. 31–52.

Other Sources

Georgia Municipal Association. *A Study of Municipal Water and Sewer Utility Rates and Practices in Georgia.* Atlanta: Georgia Municipal Association, 1965.

Howe, Charles E., and Linaweaver, F. P., Jr. *The Impact of Price on Residential Water Demand and Its Relation to System Design and Price Structures.* Washington: Resources for the Future, 1967.

Kafoglis, Milton Z. "Output of the Firm Under an Earnings Restraint," manuscript, University of Tennessee, 1968.

————. "The Public Interest in Utility Rate Structures," undated manuscript.

Pennsylvania League of Cities. *Water Utility Operations.* Harrisburg: Pennsylvania League of Cities, 1967.

UNIVERSITY OF FLORIDA MONOGRAPHS

Social Sciences

J